W9-ABP-368

In Search of the
HUMAN JESUS

ROBERT NORTH

CARMELITE MONASTERY
UNIVERSITY AVE.
NEW YORK, 10452 N. Y.

CORPUS PAPERS

CORPUS BOOKS   New York / Cleveland

232.8

N

In Search of the Human Jesus is included in CORPUS PAPERS, a series of informative studies on specific contemporary issues in Scripture, Doctrine, Morality, and Counseling.

CORPUS PAPERS

Copyright © 1969 by Robert North
Copyright © 1970 by Corpus Instrumentorum, Inc.

Library of Congress Catalog Card Number: 77-135454

All rights reserved. No part of this book may be reproduced in any form without permission from the publisher, except for brief passages included in a review appearing in a magazine or newspaper.

Contents

Preface

The man Jesus of Nazareth is Son of God, the Incarnate Word, the definitive revelation of the Father, the mediator between God and man. This is the bedrock of Christian faith.

It is also a mystery, a major mystery of the faith. Efforts to express this mystery in a meaningful and to some extent understandable way have been the concern of the Christian faithful since the first Pentecost and continue to our own day.

The history of the Church shows how vigorously the Church has always guarded against two dangers: the denial of Jesus' full humanity and the denial of his true divinity. The arguments presented in this Corpus Paper help us see that a third pitfall of equal importance has faced the Christian from the beginning and has likewise been warned against: the danger of making the humanity and divinity of Jesus two separate juxtaposed realities instead of one irreducible unity.

Very early in the life of the Church the docetist and gnostic heresies made the human Jesus a mere shadow reality and thus in effect denied the incarnation. A polemic against this viewpoint is carried on within the New Testament itself, particularly in the first epistle of John. Although this position is rarely explicitly affirmed today, many contemporary theologians believe that a subtle form of the docetist heresy exists in the practical life of believing Christians. Once they verbally confess that Jesus is true man, they go on thinking of him principally as God walking the earth in human dress, without explicitly realizing that to think of Jesus in this way is to rob his manhood of any true significance. As Karl Rahner has said, "in the ordinary life of the Christian . . . Christ has a place only as God." ("Current Problems in Christolology," *Theological Investigations* [Baltimore: Helicon, 1961], Vol. I, p. 165.)

The Arian heresy of the third century was directed against the divinity of Jesus, and it found widespread acceptance. One day, wrote Jerome, "the whole world woke up to find itself Arian." Here the error lay in calling the true divinity of Jesus into question. Or at least the terms "similar substance," "identical substance," and "self-existing substance" were not given precise meanings and a good deal of equivocation was involved. So heated did the debates initiated by the Arian controversies become that arguments used to break out in bakeries and butcher shops from Alexandria to Ephesus. Arianism was such a shock to the Christian Church, according to many twentieth-century theologians, that subsequent generations emphasized the divinity of Jesus to such an extent that, for all practical purposes, his real humanity was lost sight of. It is possibly an overreaction to the Arian heresy that has made it possible for docetism to become so subtle a danger to Christian believers.

Consequently recent experts in the field of Christology, despite the protest that they have at times provoked, have seen a greater danger to the faith in neglecting Jesus' complete and total humanity. At least they see this as a greater danger for believers than the danger of denying his divinity. The number is still legion who deny that Jesus is God.

This paper reports on some exceptionally stimulating efforts by Dutch theologians to clarify the relation between the human and the divine in Jesus. The most prominent of these theologians is already well known in America, the Dominican Edward Schillebeeckx. As the report discloses, he tends to be the most tradition-minded and moderate, critical to some degree of some of the extreme views of his colleagues. But basically he accepts and extols a proposition that must at first sight seem shocking to any Christian: "The divinity of Jesus *consists in* the perfection of his humanity." The arguments set forth by the Dutch theologians to validate this view, however, are of great depth and merit careful consideration. This proposition, which Schillebeeckx endorses, was actually proposed by the Augustinian theologian Ansfried Hulsbosch. He was stimulated to suggest this way of viewing Jesus by reflecting on the effort of Pierre Teilhard de Chardin to break down a vicious dualism between spirit and matter. Although Schillebeeckx accepts this way of expressing the divinity of Christ, he dislikes its Teilhardian genesis. But it is this link that aroused the interest of the Jesuit biblical archeologist Robert North, inasmuch as it bore a striking resemblance to some views that he had set forth in 1967 in his own study, *Teilhard and the Creation of the Soul,* and it is North's account that is provided here.

A third major contributor to the reformation of Christological teaching in The Netherlands is the Jesuit Piet Schoonenberg. His concern is to link "anti-dualist Christology" with an emphatic exposure of what he regards as the pseudo-dogma of pre-existence. I must frankly state at once that I think this is the weakest and most questionable position taken by the Dutch theologians, yet it is important that qualified students be given a chance to listen to Schoonenberg's arguments and draw their own conclusions.

Pre-existence as a dogma is indeed saved by Schoonenberg, but only as an aspect of God's eternity. There never was a *time* when Second Person was not distinct from the First as Son from Father. But that is because the first and all other moments of time are equally present to God, including the relatively late moment in which God exists as Son only in and by becoming incarnate.

It is not very clear, at least to me, how such a reformulation of pre-existence can be made to square with the Christian tradition as a whole, and in particular with the Prologue of John's Gospel. The reader would do well to study in advance the commentaries on this Prologue by Raymond Brown (Anchor Bible) and Bruce Vawter (Jerome Biblical Commentary) and compare their interpretation with that of Schoonenberg. Faith in the genuine "subsistential" existence of the Word as distinct from the Father "from the beginning" is a constant in the Christian tradition. Because of their views on this issue, Schoonenberg and Hulsbosch seem to make the reality of three distinct persons within the Godhead a meaningless assertion.

North does not defend or espouse this view, admitting that not all the doctrinal claims of the Dutch theologians can be accepted. Yet he does show a basic sympathy to their fundamental thesis, namely that Jesus' divinity consists precisely in the perfection of his humanity. I think it is of critical importance to point out, right at the start, that this basic contention seems to make the incarnation mean that man has become God rather than the other way around. Perhaps this point can be made clearer if we look at a key stacking of parallels accepted by the Dutch theologians and by North:

Living things are not matter plus life but living matter.
Men are not body plus soul but animated body.
Jesus is not man plus God but [divinized man].

The bracketed part of the final proposition is not, it is true, used by North or his Dutch sources. Yet it seems to me to be the inescapable completion of the parallels they bring forth in support of their major argument on the nature of Jesus' divinity, and in that context it seems to say that "man becomes God" and not, as the Church has traditionally expressed this truth of faith, that "God becomes man." When North was asked whether this way of completing the parallels adduced was legitimate, he admitted embarrassment, adding however, that the traditional way of speaking about the incarnation would surely not be happy with a suggested alternate, namely a "humanized God." Although I believe that "humanized God" adequately and accurately mirrors the tradition of the Church and expresses the truth that has constantly been the very center of the Christian faith, it is not to our purpose here to argue the case. The issue is raised here simply to show my own conviction that God becomes man in Jesus and my fear that the thrust of the arguments advanced in the Dutch discussion seems to imply that the man Jesus becomes divine or, to put it another way, that in Jesus man becomes God.

The text of North's summary and evaluation of the Dutch discussion is taken basically from *Theological Studies,* and we are grateful to the editor, Walter Burghardt, for granting us permission to reprint the material. The first several pages of the paper, in which North argues in defense of the theological method followed by the Dutch investigators, are taken from an article originally published in *Continuum,* and are reprinted with the permission of its editor, Justus George Lawler.

WILLIAM E. MAY

The Search for
the Human Jesus

"Render to Caesar the things that are Caesar's, and to God the things that are God's" (Mt 22:21) does not mean that there are some things that do not belong to God at all. It means rather that some things belong to a secular order of administration and others do not. This holds not merely for the political but also for the intellectual or academic order of reality. A major task of theology throughout its history has consisted in withdrawing from the sacral sphere things that either never belonged there in the first place, or had gradually ceased to belong there. What gets in there without belonging there can be summed up under the general name of superstition or magic. Obviously it was no loss to religion to be relieved of these excrescences. This never meant taking away from God anything that belonged to him. Rather it meant purifying and *increasing* what was given to God, by the very fact of transferring to Caesar what was Caesar's.

"Watering down" is a term often heard nowadays to express the dismay of devout and responsible people who once learned their theology quite well, at seeing new and especially "natural" explanations for things that they had always felt constrained to accept as part of the patrimony of faith. "The things that are God's" will inevitably include some verities so mysterious that our willingness to accept them is a true measure of our loyalty to God. *Credo quia absurdum* thus has a very legitimate sense. Only where love and trust are supremely strong, it becomes a sweet self-dedication to accept on another's word what our own intelligence and experience could never admit. But it by no means follows from this that *the more* absurdities we assent to with the invocation of God's name, the more we love and trust him. There is no virtue and loyalty in accepting implausibilities on any trusted friend's word except in the exact measure in which we are sure he *demands* it.

We might provisionally say that it is the function of authority and tradition in the Church to lay down the measure in which God demands the sacrifice of our understanding; and it is the function of theology to go on from there.

Theology, like any other science or branch of scholarship, does not provide its own data, but supplies a reasoned framework for the facts *given* to it. The data of theology, as its name implies, include whatever is known about God. We might express this differently and accurately by saying that the data of theology arise from "God's revealing himself." If there is a God, then every existing thing gives some clue to him, and the whole creation is thus a revelation of him. This portion of the data is dealt with by the branch of scholarship called natural theology.

Really we should call it *just* theology. The object of any human or natural knowledge is what can *naturally* be known about it. Thus there is no need to say "natural physics" or "natural astronomy" to make clear that we are not taking into account what might be known about these things by miracle.

Then why do we reverse our procedure in presuming that our theology is not just "natural" unless we say so expressly? The reason is that theology is science about God. And it is precisely God who would or must be responsible for anything men might know *otherwise* than "naturally" about him or anything else. Hence it is not altogether unmethodical if those who believe in a "supernatural" knowledge generally say *just* "theology" to mean whatever can be known of God in *any* way, and especially in the ways that are uniquely reserved to him.

Just as theology does not produce its own data, so it can never abandon or forget them. It must constantly correct and criticize itself by going back to reexamine the concrete facts given to it from outside itself. This is the truth still enshrined in the somewhat dated proverb that the physicist or scientist must "keep his feet on the ground." Theology as scholarship can never relinquish to any parliament or body of administrators the reexamination of the data on which it depends. This must be its own responsibility. Otherwise it will cease to be theology, just as surely as physics would cease to be physics if it began to draw its information from Aristotle or Einstein instead of the good earth.

Plainly there is need of authority and law to keep the data of all the sciences available to their lawful users. Any scholar must welcome and depend upon those organs of public welfare that preserve his data unimpaired. The conservation-structures of the worshipping community (which for a Catholic means the Church and her magisterium) are the only practical and possible way for the data of revelation to be preserved and made available to the theologian. Indeed, a large part of his work must lie in the vindication of these conservation-forces. But this does not mean that he can ever renounce or hand over to them his duty of reexamining his own data.

The data of theology include preeminently whatever God may have revealed about himself by miraculous interventions. Yet from this source even the most strictly "supernatural theology" draws only a small proportion of its total data. Even the relatively few theologians who with Karl Barth reject any natural knowledge of God must still expend the major share of their effort on reconciling or correcting what nature has to say on the subject. But for most theologians, the few propositions that we take as coming from God directly are flanked and pummeled and clarified by myriad relevant propositions known naturally from the book of creation.

Since the natural data of theology are drawn from anywhere and everywhere in the whole created universe knowable to us, they are coextensive with the material universe. Thus the thing studied by physics is identical with the thing studied by theology.

Despite the vast disproportion between theology and physics . . . however much physics relates to the measurable while theology is concerned with what can be known only in faith: still each of these two sciences deals in its own way with the same thing, Cosmic Reality. . . . When the physicist in face of the complexity of matter confesses his ignorance, he attests that same yearning for a tranquilizing synthesis which characterizes the theologian's search for an explanation of the .revelation of God in Christ.[1]

Both physics and theology draw their information from a "given," which consists of any and every material thing anywhere. Of course they focus on different "aspects" or even different *contents* within the same "given/*datum.*" Theology asks the atom or galaxy only what it can tell of God. But it must not be imagined that even God's revelation comes to believers apart from material objects:

God is nowhere accessible otherwise than in his created mani-festations. . . . The world of human experience is our only access to that type of truth, which however is not a curtaining horizon. Human-corporeal perception is the basis of all our knowledge, even precisely where it manifests the transcendent. The known earthly situation is also our only access to explicit and actual knowledge of other eventual realities. For this very reason God's revelation happens in a human happening, and faith cannot be detached from our experience in a tangible world among fellow-men.[2]

Even if there is any "spirit to spirit" communication from God to the "soul" (and this is highly doubtful), there has never been the slightest evidence of such a thing not indispensably involving material images. And the normal ways with which the term *revelation* has always been primarily associated are material bodies speaking with a material voice.

Since therefore the virtual totality of our knowledge of God comes through material things, it is possible that with a radical alteration in our understanding of ma-terial processes there will come an alteration in our un-derstanding of what God is revealing to us by them. In a former day, to produce light out of darkness or be heard from another planet must surely have seemed a revela-tion of the power of God. And so it is, but in a way which today would be understood as due entirely and *also* to natural human ingenuity. It is one of those things that have been "rendered to Caesar."

The material identity of the objects of theology and physics as "Cosmic Reality," which we quoted above from the Augustinian Hulsbosch, is taken as the point of departure for a stimulating and somewhat terrifying new Christology. The same issue of *Tijdschrift voor Theologie* offers the reactions of the Dominican Schillebeeckx and the Jesuit Schoonenberg to Hulsbosch's bold hypothesis that the divinity of Jesus is seen to consist in the perfection or elevation of his humanity.

Soul-Body Unity and God-Man Unity

Hulsbosch's formula takes as its point of departure an assurance regarding the body-soul relation in man which happens to be identical with one that we defended in a recent volume.[3] Hulsbosch specifically links the problem with the name of Teilhard de Chardin, and has in fact specialized in Teilhard's thought and unmistakably shows its influence.[4]

So daringly new an approach to the perennial Christological mystery is of such sufficient intrinsic urgency to merit presentation. But our goal is proximately to evaluate the extent to which it really is, as claimed, a corollary of the evolutionist body-soul relation. To the extent that this claim is valid, our own position is weakened or strengthened by being wedded to the reformulation of a dogma of incalculably greater delicacy.

That Hulsbosch chose to link his true and valid conclusions with an ephemeral evolutionism is a pity, we will see Schillebeeckx saying. Although he meant by this chiefly to accept and bolster Hulsbosch's conclusion, he in fact thereby asserted that the validity of the evolutionism was independent of whatever judgment one might make about the Christology that, to a considerable extent, he shares with Hulsbosch. Perhaps not all will agree that such complex issues warrant such a simple compartmentalizing. Here is the relevant passage:

Frankly I rather regret personally that he [Hulsbosch] chose to tie down his exposition inside an evolutionary framework. This outlook, with its inherent thorough-going "monistic" psychology *(Anthropologie)* is still doubtful in many points. Such a background can only be a stumbling block for any fully new explanation of the already far too delicate problem of the man Jesus. Did p. 254 really have to say that even Jesus is "the unfolding of possibilities lying latent in matter itself"? Precisely over any such "unfolding" at all there is currently a ferment among philosophers and theologians; we are far from any consensus on definite basic positions. Everything about evolution is still in a very experimental stage. Discussion bound to be evoked by Hulsbosch's new Christology could have been kept more serene if he had not coupled his first presentation of it so inexorably to an evolutionist outlook, legitimate enough in itself but still in need of clarification on some really basic issues. Admittedly he drew his own new insight about Christ from this evolutionary environment, which thus self-evidently forms the context of his whole theological exposition. For himself it is thus not just one of various possibilities for an introductory paragraph, but is the veritable *Sitz im Leben* of his new interpretation.[5]

We may regard the above advertence to the "discussion bound to be evoked" as an invitation to foster this dialogue.

The Hulsbosch Comparison Formula: Known as Man, Confessed as God

"Jesus is *known* as man," Hulsbosch proclaims in his title, "but *confessed to be* Son of God." This is not to imply that Jesus is not known to be Son of God. But there is a difference. The burden of his article consists in claiming that if the divinity of Jesus consists in some separate reality juxtaposed beside his humanity, then it is irrelevant to us, and Jesus can never be the revelation of God to us. Because the true man Jesus *is* the revelation of God to us, his divinity can never be grasped as any other thing than a feature of his humanity. It is the humanity itself which is elevated by being divine. "The divinity of Christ consists in the perfection of his humanity."

The unity of any man's being is ever more seen to demand rectifying current dualistic concepts of the soul as a *thing* distinct from another *thing* which is the body. Teilhard rightly ascribed our spiritual or conscious activities to an evolutionally organized "inner face" of matter itself, rather than to any component distinct from matter. "Should not the same revision also take place in regard to the unity of Christ?" asks Hulsbosch. "The early Fathers were already familiar with the idea that the unity of Christ shows a resemblance to man's own inner unity" (p. 251).

If those Fathers failed to spell out this parallel as explicitly as we would like, this can easily be accounted for by the monophysite menace. They would undoubtedly have agreed that the unity of God and man in Christ is as great as the unity of body and soul in man. But today we cannot tolerate the notion of one thing which is a body and a second thing which is a soul combining into a third thing which is a man. No more can we tolerate a "third reality" combined of the divine and the human in Christ.

We know from the certitude of experience, not our immediate personal experience but the shared experience of the human community, that Jesus was true man. We also confess, or "know as a mystery of faith," that he was God. But it does not follow from this that we know, either as experience or by faith, *how* while being man he can be God. We tend to think of this prerogative as two things within him, just as we tend to think of our soul as a thing in us distinct from another thing which is our body. Hence it would seem that Hulsbosch is in the right, more than Schillebeeckx is willing to admit, for claiming a relevance of body-soul evolutionism to the Christological problem.

A scholarly approach to the soul or to the divinity of Christ or to any other problem should begin with the *facts* which we have in our hands either experimentally or as genuine *data* of our faith. Theoretical *explanations* of the data, even if embodied in sublime or tradition-bound formulas, should be utilized as a point of *arrival* rather than departure.

In the soul-body relation, the *given* is that I know myself to be a material being, *and* I know myself to have (in common with other men) certain activities called "spiritual" and perceptibly surpassing the activities of other kinds of matter. "This material me also has a soul" is *not* part of the given experience; much less is the *nature* of that "soul." Rather from the given facts four possibilities open out, and only *speculation* can enable me to make a choice among them.

(1) The supra-animal activities of man must be attributed to some *separate thing* inside him which he does not have in common with the brute or stone. This, no matter how you refine it, is what Plato called a pure spirit (i.e. an "angel") imprisoned within the cage of bodily flesh. If this is what people mean when they speak of their "soul," then it must be fearlessly proclaimed that they are *not* describing any reality which they haxe *experienced,* but are passing on in slogan-form the result of someone else's keen but fallible reasonings.

(2) Equally a deductive hypothesis based on experience, not a datum of experience itself, is the Thomist claim that the soul is "form" (really "shape") of the body. The fact that this is a vastly more realistic and acceptable ascription does not mean that it ceases to be speculation and becomes experience. It enjoys a certain enigmatic support from faith;[6] but the "defined dogma" asserts ultimately only that there is in man no "separate thing" called a soul. The speculative philosophical explanation of how this can be is left free.

(3) A third hypothesis, that of the ancient materialists, was no less inferential. Human activities apparently "spiritual" in the sense of transcending animality were de-

clared to be just an illusion, and were wholly accounted for by the visible and measurable aspects of matter itself.

(4) There is a fourth hypothesis, really on the same footing whether we like it or not, and whether we consider it ultimately different from the third or not. This is Teilhard's claim that there really are spiritual activities and they are due to an inherent quality of matter itself, but a quality which in smaller units escapes observation and is only observed as "consciousness" after its units are combined in complex organized trillions.

In all this, the only admissible scientific attitude is to inquire not "What can there be inside a human being, different from matter, that enables him to think?"[7] but "How can we explain the experienced datum that a *material thing thinks?*" In exactly the same way, Hulsbosch insists that the "given" *datum* of experience, passionately defended by faith and tradition, is "Jesus was a man." An *unusual* man, a special *kind* of man, even *more* than an ordinary man is also included in the datum. In fact it can even be called a datum that he was God, if it is recognized how much more obscurely and tentatively this is expressed in the earliest sources of our information. But *how* it is possible for a man to be unmistakably man and yet simultaneously also God, is not part of the datum. It is a *mystery,* which must be "sounded," and for which an explanation must be *sought.* Or at least so Hulsbosch thinks, and we think he is right. Here is how he outlines his program.

The history of Christology is at bottom a search for the unity of that person who became known as man and confessed as the Son of God. The Church in her confession has always held fast to the unity of these so diverse components. But in speaking of "two natures," she has called forth a tension that has persisted until today. In fact today it is felt more keenly than ever. What is inevitably conjured up is the image of a Christ divided into two layers (p. 250).

Hulsbosch here invokes an earlier article by Schoonenberg denying that a Christ divided between two layers has anything to say any more to the people of our day. We experience around us vague and unformulated but unmistakable revivals of Arianism and adoptionism. On the one hand we eagerly emphasize the human life of Jesus. On the other hand, we find nothing in our knowledge of reality enabling us to combine in a single formula the transcendence of God with the historical man Jesus of Nazareth.

Christ Involved in Evolution?

People who persist in clamoring that Christ is a mere man cannot effectively be refuted by merely repeating traditional formulas. When they reject the "validity" of such a formula, they are not saying anything against its truth. They merely find in it nothing relevant to human existence. Hulsbosch admits that in some few cases the New Testament itself, as far as common sense can judge, portrays Christ as just a man.

People today are, however, willing to accept the place of Christ in evolution. First there was matter without life, then there was plant and animal life, and thirdly there was man. Because of the work of Teilhard de Chardin, the coexistence of the human race in the person of Christ can now be called a fourth phase of evolution.

Here Hulsbosch seems to be tacitly approving Teilhard's theory of "continuity through discontinuity," effected by "critical thresholds." Continuous quantitative input produces at certain levels a qualitative change, a new and different reality, just as water by boiling becomes steam. Teilhard further theorized that the whole human race is at present on the verge of another upward step, a threshold no less critical than the first appearance of mankind itself. Today humanity is in the throes of a greater unification with and in itself, by convergence on an "Omega Point" alleged somehow to involve Christ in the created universe.

Such Omega theorizing really issues in a union of divinity with humanity in the "Body of Christ." This name has customarily been understood to mean the *mystical* body. But some exegetes like Barnabas Ahern have been claiming that Christ's *physical* body is intended here.[8] In either case, the union of divinity with matter can be called parallel to the union of spiritual with bodily reality in man, or of life with organic matter.

Hulsbosch here aptly alludes to a misconception in the current impasse between "Vitalism" and biological mechanism. The assumption of both sides is that "living matter" must be either *"just* matter" or "matter *plus* life." It is *not* matter plus life; it is materiality itself attaining to a fuller unfolding. This view respects both the unique value of life and the unity of the human being.

Man is distinguished from the lower animals by his capacity of reflex knowledge. For the explanation of the whole unique subjectivity of man there is postulated the existence of a rational soul different from the material body. Traditional theological terminology even includes unhesitant allusion to the separation of soul and body in death. That notion of a "separated soul" is encountering in our day ever fiercer resistance. We cannot regard the essential unity of man as sufficiently secured in any system which makes him the combination of one material and one spiritual component. The solution is precisely as in the vitalism controversy. Just as living matter is nothing other than the unfolding of non-living matter into a higher phenomenological form, why cannot we also say that man's being is [a similarly discontinuous] unfolding of animal life, and that the intellectual life of man belongs to the variety of forms in which it is possible for matter to appear? (p. 252)

This view had already been put forward in an earlier article.[9]

We know the difference between living and nonliving matter. In the same way there is also matter with sensitive activity and matter with intellective activity. By this we mean simply that we may not drag any static element into the unfolding of reality, whether we call such a static element "life" or "matter" or "soul." It is matter itself which is appearing in ever new forms; it becomes ever different, raises itself to ever higher levels. . . . The living being is not matter plus life, but living matter. Man is not matter plus spirit, but—at any rate, in a definite sector of his bodiliness—animated matter capable of those activities which we call spiritual.

The "Life" Cannot be Other than What Lives

Hulsbosch then (p. 253) bolsters his argument by taking up the point which independently furnished the major thesis of my recent volume on Teilhard:

We hear it said that God at a given moment after the origin of life on earth took an animal body and inserted into it a spiritual soul. At first sight this seems like a good explanation. But upon closer look we find ourselves up against scarcely acceptable consequences. In a certain sense God would be making inroads into the innerworldly order of things. Precisely in the very thing which makes man man, the evolution of life on earth would be registering failure. It keeps on running along a sidetrack of bodily life; but in his veritable being, man would not belong to the matter from which he took his origin. At the point where a foreign element intrudes, man would have to be seen as a juxtaposition of two heterogeneous items. But if we consent to regard man's intellectual life rather as something for which matter itself contains the capability, any threat of duality is surmounted and man can really be grasped as a unity.

This reasoning can be continued with regard to Jesus of Nazareth. First of all, Hulsbosch faces frankly the fact that we seem headed toward the conclusion that Jesus was a mere man. "Regarding living being, we have said that 'life' must not be sought in some separate element that is *different* from the inorganic matter in which it took its rise. Regarding man, we have claimed that the presence of intellectual activities in no way forces the assumption of an immaterial soul as a reality distinct from the material body. In both cases we have progressed toward a better view of the real unity of the being."

Turning then to Jesus: since Scripture insists firmly that he is a man taken from among us, must we not then abandon the notion that his special prerogatives differentiating him from other men are to be reduced to a separate divine principle distinct from his human nature? Hulsbosch finds that such an alleged divine principle would be just as alien to the true unified being as the allegedly separate spiritual soul. In both cases there would be something brought in from outside, making the person of Jesus doubly a juxtaposition of two realities, the divine nature being admittedly even far more heterogeneous than the human soul.

Must we not here also say, Hulsbosch continues (p. 254), that matter itself includes among its potencies that of being bearer of the activities which characterize Jesus? In that case the prerogatives which set Jesus apart from other men should be called "divine" in the sense of godlike. "As long as we are really serious about insisting on the personal unity of the man Jesus, we must say that here too we have an unfolding of the capabilities which lay latent within matter."

This was the utterance that so shocked even Schillebeeckx, despite his warm approval for the thesis that it rather irreproachably summarizes. Perhaps we might permit ourselves more distress at the word "new" in the sentence which follows: "Jesus is a man; He is man in a new and higher way." As will appear from the reasonings of Husbosch and of his two sympathetic critics, and as is even more prominent in Teihard, Christ represents not really a "new" or higher level to which mankind after a long time was raised. Rather, Christ is the *primordial* man, the exemplar for whom the whole of creation exists, and in whom chiefly it is the image of God. Of course, Hulsbosch's word "new" is not meant to deny this, only to express "different" and "higher" in a time-bound hierarchy of evolutional realizations.

Jesus is this "new" man above all in his glorification, which made evident that in him manhood had crossed a higher threshold. This mode of viewing, Hulsbosch avers, would doubtless give full expression to the unity of Christ. But the price really seems to be too high. He would no longer be seen as the Son, one with the Father in his divine nature. He would be just the human vehicle of an unusual grace.

Relation of Evolution to Chalcedon

The second major area in which Hulsbosch is sympathetic to modern distaste for aging theological tags concerns the hypostatic union. Before following him here, we might introduce this bridging part of Schillebeeckx's evaluation (p. 274):

Hulsbosch's study of the unity of Jesus Christ, "who is *known* as man and *confessed* as Son of God," fights on two fronts. Against alarming modern tendencies to downgrade Christ to the level of an ordinary man among fellow men, doubtless prophetically superendowed but in a line with other religious geniuses, he reacts by striking a blow for the primacy of love of God, though seeing it as bound up with love of men. But he also voices vehement criticism of traditional views prompted by such dogmatic formulas as "two natures in one person" or "hypostatic union." He in fact claims to see a thread of continuity between the two excesses he combats: precisely because our experience of reality cannot live with a "split-level Christ" which he himself rejects, some conclude that Christ cannot rationally be conceived except as an *ordinary* man, so that nothing has been essentially altered by his coming into our world. The latter view reduces ultimately to theorizing about the Chalcedon dogma "true God and true man" without due concern for one of its two items, though it had been precisely the Council's concern to deny any *combining* or consequent duality of Godhead and manhood in Christ. Hulsbosch combats the modern leveling tendency by purging from traditional Christology just that which modern man can no longer integrate in his outlook. By defending untouchably the recaptured original intention of the "true God and true man" formula, he aims efficiently to hijack *(opvangen)* for orthodoxy a good part of dissenting modern views. In our day there is no probative force in censures, anathemas, or invocations of authority; what is true can and must make sense to modern man when set forth in its fulness. Our belief is no abracadabra. In what has been revealed to us we must be able to recognize what our heart had so long craved: revelation is at its deepest the joyous discovery that God has in fact effected in Christ the very thing our spirit had yearned for, redemption. Thus revelation is inextricably bound up with the meaningfulness of human existence. If really then modern man can find no place in his life for "two natures but one person," we must reappraise what this formula really meant to impose as dogma. This attitude does not presuppose that we maneuver public opinion as the ultimate criterion of whether or not to accept the datum of faith. But it does play an indispensable role in our striving toward assigning to the unconditionally preaccepted aim of the dogma its proper place in the total framework of our human experience of faith.

To this we will say a fervent amen. Well then, according to Hulsbosch (p. 254), the Chalcedon dogma of the hypostatic union bears an unmistakably static imprint.

"Until recently it was normal in theology to speak of Christ in such a way that any development in him from an earthly to a heavenly state of being was purely a side issue. It did not need to clutter up whatever had to be said about the hypostatic union. Such inflexibleness is alien to the New Testament, which plainly reckons with a genuine human development in Christ. However much closer current theology clings to the New Testament data than before, the basic problem of the combining of human and divine in one person has not vanished. The more we recognize true man in the biblical Jesus, the more we must keep on confessing that he is simultaneously Son of God. The more we learn about his true manhood, the more difficult such a confession becomes; and that is scarcely a mere question of feelings."

Some Problems of Christ's Knowledge

Hulsbosch would be only too happy to go along with Aquinas when he says (*Sum. theol.* 3, q.9, a.1, ad lm) that we cannot admit a genuinely divine knowledge within the human soul of Christ without thereby destroying the proper operations of each respective nature within him, and indeed destroying any human knowledge within him at all, since the knowledge he did have would have no human faculty proportioned to it. But how then can modern theology struggle to base the self-consciousness of Jesus in his divine person? He has the self-awareness of being Son of God, but the mode of this awareness in him bears the features of human self-consciousness. "Can we theologically tolerate the formula that Jesus in his human self-awareness knows that he is Son of God?[10] Impossible!" Here Hulsbosch is not arguing either as a scientist or as a dilettante against trained theologians. He is asking theologians to be consistent with their own convictions.

"Whatever awareness Jesus had of being God's Son, as a human awareness it can never be the *adequate* reflection of a divine subjectivity. The personality of Jesus cannot be deeper than the depth of the human subjectivity which he experiences in his human self-consciousness" (p. 255). It is not obvious why this should be so, as we will explain after a moment. But it is also not quite obvious whether Hulsbosch is fully subscribing to this view, or merely setting forth along with its tragic flaw a modern outlook with which he is in fundamental sympathy. At any rate, he pauses to consider an objection handled by textbook traditions. He had said that a human awareness could not reflect a divine subjectivity *adequately,* i.e. fully, in every way. But it is said that a *genuine* though not adequate reflection would suffice, just as in the beatific vision of ordinary men a comprehensive knowledge of God is not prerequisite to a genuine personal relation with him. Hulsbosch denies the parity. No more of God is in fact known in the beatific vision than the subjective experience of the viewer can support, and there are facets of God's being which simply remain irrelevant to the blessed; God is not there attained in his proper transcendence but only in the created reality of human experience. "Similarly Christ in his human consciousness cannot attain the divine transcendence; the personal self-awareness which he can attain is trammeled within created measures. When Jesus is aware of himself as the Son, that admittedly includes an altogether special relationship to God. But that is portrayed as only gradually and not absolutely from the start distinct from the relationship which other men have to God."

Here there seems to be a weakness in his argument. Apparently Hulsbosch is claiming that as a theologian he can deny that Jesus experienced a certain kind of relationship to God. In order to make this denial, the theologian himself must have a certain kind of grasp of the type of relationship which he is denying. But if a theologian can envision such a relationship to God even in order to deny it, then it is not clear why Jesus in his human consciousness could not have "envisioned" it, i.e. been aware of it as a mysterious thing mysteriously belonging to him. Thus it would not be true that "Christ in his human consciousness cannot attain the divine transcendence." Hulsbosch might well answer: "Perhaps theoretically it *could* be so, but Scripture just does not describe it that way." Even if such an argument from silence could be admitted as conclusive in the present speculations, it would seem that he has overstated his case at this point. But it is not clear that this detail is fundamental or indispensable to his thesis.

Christ is God by Being Man in a Special Way

The problem is next taken up from a wholly different point of view. The Son of God became man. That is revealed to us as a saving mystery. "Actuation of that salvation can take place only in the sector of the human. This man is Son of God in that this man is in contact with God in a way that separates him from ordinary men. But this can mean nothing other than a special way of being-man, since the whole actuality of the mystery still lies precisely in the sector of the human. In reflecting on the mystery, it is doubtless convenient to set the two natures over against each other, but a divine nature juxtaposed beside the human gets us nowhere." Here (p. 255) follows what Schillebeeckx (p. 276) cites in full as the kernel of the Hulsbosch thesis to which he gives his own "one hundred percent approbation":

The divine nature of Jesus is relevant to the saving mystery only insofar as it alters and elevates the human nature. And whatever that is must be called a new mode of being man. We keep turning around in the same circle: the divine nature is here irrelevant except insofar as it elevates the human nature. To the extent that it does this, it puts us in contact with a *human* reality. When one says "Jesus is, besides man, also God," such an "also God" cannot form part of the salvation reality. The mystery borrows its whole reality from what belongs to the human sphere.

Despite the impressiveness of Schillebeeckx's approval, it is not altogether clear here why the divine nature, even if juxtaposed in dualist fashion, could not have the effect of elevating the human nature. Or at least one would have welcomed a further spelling out of this argument. We may notice here the cautious and sympathetic terms by which Schillebeeckx (p. 275) in fact dissociates himself from Hulsbosch's rejection of the hypostatic union formula:

Because our human thinking is factually determined by history, it is inadmissible to stay simon-pure in a vacuum by just repeating old dogmas and reaffirming their materiality. Mere repetition of identical words and formulas that grew up in and out of another era may well bypass exactly the relevance that the dogma has for our day. Our knowledge cannot gaze out upon history like a landscape, because we are not above it. In *our* situation the fifth-century dogmatic formulas are experienced in faith in a different way than earlier. Thereby the past itself becomes different for us, and becomes awakened to new life. For example, a Jewish-Christian's understanding of "Son of God" was nuanced somewhat differently from that of a Christian from pagan background, even though both were expressing rightly the exclusive relation of the man Jesus to God.

Hulsbosch is extremely sensitive to this law of human life. His aim is to give a genuine interpretation to the dogma of the hypostatic union, in such a way that while holding firmly to the word of God and consequently to the basic intention of the Church dogma, it can become really operative in a *Weltanschauung* of modern psychology. One may raise the question whether his new explanation of the relation between the truly divine and the truly human in the person of Christ meets head-on the essential nub of the dogmatic datum. One may even wonder whether his article rightly expresses the traditional content of the "hypostatic union" concept. Or is it—on the basis of expressions which in fact can all too easily be found in our dogma textbooks—somewhat tendentiously distorted in such a way that it can be more comfortably demythologized?

Postponing until later what Schillebeeckx has to say more positively in defensive reappraisal of Chalcedon, we may here note that the article by which Piet Schoonenberg expresses his reaction to Hulsbosch is more tolerant of his attack on the hypostatic formula.[11]

I think he has achieved something worthwhile in forcing a reappraisal of the question [but I am not quite ready to agree with his answer that duality in Christ can be evaded only by making his divinity an "aspect" of the Father's own.] Instead, I will propose some elements which still have to be mulled over, in view of an eventual stance. It seems to me difficult to transpose directly into Hulsbosch's categories the dogma of Chalcedon, which incidentally does not itself exclude the historicity of Jesus' human and even (in the way explained by Rahner) divine nature, nor does it ever say that the sole person in Christ is the divine person of the Word. *DS* 302 says we must "acknowledge one and the same Christ, Son, Lord, only-begotten. . . in two natures 'running together' in one person and one hypostasis." This formula evokes rather "divine-human" than just "divine" as description of the person of Christ.

Schoonenberg here supports the view that the divine person of the Word in becoming man becomes more person, in that it takes on an I-thou relation to the Father.[12] He rather doubts, though he does not exclude, that this I-thou relation can be equated with a nonhypostatic self-revealing Presence of the Father in Christ. But he agrees that more indirectly the Hulsbosch formula may represent the Chalcedon content.

Origen Distorting John Caused Two Extremes

We must recognize that every human utterance is situation-bound. Schoonenberg bluntly lays it on the line that the Chalcedon situation was one in which John's straightforward declaration that "the Word *became* flesh" had been transformed by Origen into "the Word *took on* flesh." This reformulation brought with it a never-ending tension between Arian subordinationism and Sabellian modalism, between Nestorian "two persons" and Monophysite "one nature" (p. 305):

That tension could be harnessed by the Councils only in hypostatizing Son and Spirit, and the wonder is that they never took the further step of Trinitarian Pre-existence later worked out by theologians. . . . Hulsbosch claims to have preserved the *NT* datum equally well but in a pre-Origen situation, much as one might claim to transpose mathematical formulas into a non-Euclidean system. But it is not all that easy. The fact that such a formulation was possible before Origen does not mean that it is possible in today's situation. If Chalcedon succeeded in making explicit what was really latent in the *NT*, then after being once recognized it can never simply be locked up in a closet and ignored. Similarly, for example, even if *dato non concesso* humanity at first knew God only implicitly, it could never return to any such merely implicit knowledge. Must we say that in the same way we cannot turn back the clock on the divine hypostasis in Jesus? [The answer will have to involve, first, that Pre-existence as commonly understood *without* reference to Incarnation was a sidetrack; secondly, the Church's demand of hypostasis *could* conceivably have been situation-bound; thirdly] a positive proof is required that the definitive saving revelation of God in Christ *could not* have been realized in his very mode of being man. . . . The ultimate question becomes whether human nature is so *capax infiniti, capax Dei* that it can itself in Jesus "express" an infinite God. Perhaps Hulsbosch can seek a proof of this in what he has already drawn from the Bible about man as image of God. . . . But how can we avoid passing to a similar divinity of all men, a myth of Jesus as simply man? . . . Perhaps his Being-for-others can be shown to have an absoluteness whereby he as man is for all both Lord and Servant as God's infinite revelation and presence.

We will notice later what here worries Schoonenberg about reducing Christ to merely one of various divinizings of man, and similar expressions of Baur and Barth.

Cyril: The Human Measures Out the Divine

We have given extended comments of Schillebeeckx and Schoonenberg as a coda to Hulsbosch' own exposition of two objections drawn from the modern mentality against current Christological formulations. One is biological and one is soteriological. He finds them very cogent. But he sets them forth as a challenge. They are not the last word on the question. Yet a direct attack on them is scarcely feasible. There lies before us only the possibility of a thoroughgoing reappraisal of the whole problem. Hulsbosch sets about this (p. 256) by invoking some relevant items from an earlier research of his on Cyril of Alexandria.[13]

Against a reproach about how he distinguishes the natures in Christ, Cyril replies: "In our opinion, there is just one Son, and he has one nature, even though with it he has taken on flesh that has a true soul. For, as I observed, the human is become of him, and we think no otherwise of him than that in the same manner he is God as well as man." The words "one nature" here can be and have been misunderstood. Reference to flesh and true soul are sufficient indication that the other nature too is represented. But what Cyril is focusing on is the one nature, because the divine nature of the Logos takes on the human in order to manifest itself. The human remains a created reality, but becomes nevertheless the means for the divine nature of the Word to manifest itself. Cyril says that Christ is "in the same way God as well as man," "same way" being undoubtedly the human way: the concrete human perceptible form of Christ encompasses his being-God as well as his being-man. The divine is of itself without limit, but appears under human "measures," *metra*. . . . Cyril's position that Christ is in the same human measure God as well as man, sound in itself, can be taken in two ways: the old conciliar way, and the new way that I am proposing here.

For Cyril (p. 257), the divine that is of its nature unlimited is limited by the measure of the human into which it is poured like water into a vessel. Admittedly not Cyrillan, but better, would be the claim that the "measure" is not distinct from the thing measured; Christ is not a man *in* whom appears the presence of God; that would make of him a *mere* man and play havoc with the dogma. Rather the man as such *is* the presence of God. Because the man Christ remains a true creature revealing God by his whole human personality, creation as a whole is thereby also a manifestation of God, though in lesser and varying degrees.

This dictum, "the human is the measure in which the divine appears," is supported by Schillebeeckx (pp. 276–77) as the only rational approach to the mystery of Christ:

Since 1953 I have firmly opposed the formulation "Christ is God and man," and also the confusing expression "the man Jesus is God." In this I was in the good company of Aquinas, *Summa* 3, 16, 11 ad 1: *"Vera: Christus, secundum quod homo, habet gratiam unionis. Non: Christus, secundum quod homo, est Deus."* The proper formula would be "Jesus

Christ is the Son of God *in humanity*." The deepest sense of revelation is that God reveals himself in humanity. We cannot seek farther, above or beneath the man Jesus, his being-God. The divinity must be perceptible *in* his humanity itself: "he who sees me, sees the Father." The human form of Jesus *is* the revelation of God. Expressions such as "Jesus besides being man is also God" evacuate the deepest meaning of the Incarnation. Christ could be no revelation of God for us if *besides* the man Jesus we still needed a revelation of his [divine] "nature"—which in any case would then have to manifest itself in a *created* form. Thus the mystery lies neither beyond nor beneath the man Jesus, but in his being-man itself. Hulsbosch says rightly that "the human is the measure in which the divine appears." The divine, remaining what it is, is perceived in the measure of the human. To this formula Thomas could have subscribed: "the human measure is the mode in which God appears upon earth." Thus we do not have present a man, Jesus, in whom is realized a presence of God which is *distinct* from him. The man-Jesus himself *is* the presence of God.

God is nowhere accessible otherwise than in his created manifestations. This position of Hulsbosch, however much overlooked by theologians, seems to me irreproachable. The world of human experience is the *only* access to that type of truth, even though it is not a curtaining horizon. Human-corporeal perception is the basis of all our knowledge, even precisely when it manifests the transcendent. The known earthly situation is also our only access to explicit and actual knowledge of other eventual realities. For this very reason God's revelation happens in a human happening, and faith cannot be detached from our experience in a tangible world among fellow men.

If Christ is God, we know this only out of his mode of being man. It must be clear from his human situation: He must be man in a different and absolutely unique way. And when we have said that, we have said everything that can be said about Christ. We have no further anything to look for either beyond or deeper than his being man, such as *"Besides* this being-man, there is also a God Jesus." The "besides" is altogether out of place. Indeed, it is contrary to the whole of Christian tradition—a point which Hulsbosch seems to have missed, thus creating a straw man to attack.

Schillebeeckx (p. 277) continues that Aquinas, while maintaining the "one person, two natures," and denying a "human person" in Christ, never uses careless expressions implying that the personal subjectivity of Jesus is something beyond or other than what the man Jesus himself as subject is (*Sum. theol.* 3, q. 2, a. 2, ad 2m; *On John,* Lecture 1, 7). "The Word is man in that manner in which everyone else is man, namely, as subject of humanity (bearer of 'human nature')." The basis of the personal humanity of Jesus is not the divine person but "the human nature" (*Sum. theol.* 3, q. 3, a. 1, ad 3m). This man himself *is* the person of the Son of God (3, 2, 10c), so that in him humanity itself attains an unimaginable fulfilment (3, q. 3, a. 1, ad 1m: *"non Deus sed homo perficitur")*. Thomas calls this person pre-existent, there speaking of Christ not *simpliciter* but as the same person rooted in the divine nature, that is, the divine Son (3, q. 3, a. 1, ad 3m). Looking at the *term* of a dogmatic development, whereby of three divine persons only the second became man, he sees this presupposed in *the man Jesus:* "For him, a man who is not simultaneously person is unthinkable; not even in Christ can a nature subsist impersonally" (3, q. 16, a. 12, ad 1m). "Jesus does not possess human nature *minus* the human person; rather the human person is identically the person of the Divine Word; there is no question here of a one plus a one making a two" (p. 278; *Quaestio disputata de unione Verbi* 2, ad 2m; *Sum. theol.* 3, q. 3, a. 1, ad 2m). The unlimited God himself can appear in the limited measure of the human; God is before us in a human mode, "the Word himself is personally man" (*De unione Verbi* 2, rendering *quasi* not "as if" but "so that he is in fact").

Cajetan soberly but unhesitatingly paraphrases this "The Word himself is a human person."[14]

These scholastic refinements, despite their static speculativeness, urges Schillebeeckx (p. 279), show that the person is not a refinement extrinsic to the nature; the nature is the content or the mode of being of the person. Hence the proper subjectivity of Jesus Christ is a human subjectivity in which God the Son manifests himself personally. We must speak of the person of the man Jesus according to the human expressions by which this person reveals himself to his fellow men in Palestine and in the Gospels. Only because in this man something absolutely unique is perceptible could the Church be led to her notion of hypostatic union. But we can only understand what this formula means to her by living through those human experiences by means of which she attained it. Our modern mentality can rightly bracket as myth whatever kind of "inner-divine hypostases" are not perceived *within* the humanity of Jesus as the implication or consequence of its uniqueness. What Hulsbosch calls a "new" approach is by Schillebeeckx called more properly a retracing of the same living approach the Church herself went through, as against a lifeless and misleading parroting of ready-made formulas. Even the formulas of the *NT* itself do not give us the facts of Jesus' life directly, but only as worked over by the nascent Christology of the primitive community's faith.[15]

Creation Contains God without Pantheism

Leaving one further aspect of Schillebeeckx's critique for later consideration, we may here return to Hulsbosch's own expression of his case (p. 258):

In his quality of subject, every man is in some sense the midpoint of the universe. He knows always from within his own subjectivity and finds himself confronted by everything in his environment. In this sense he is the dead center of all reality and stands midway among all men. The universe and mankind confront him insofar as he knows them. "Insofar as he knows them" is the expression of a limitation not merely on the material contents of his knowledge but also on his mode of knowing. He does not know all things, and the number of other men he does not know is vastly greater than the ones he does; but this is less significant than the deficiencies with which he knows what he does know.

Hulsbosch goes on to show how reality is in fact itself affected by its interplay with the knowing subject, and is known differently by different men or by animals. Our mode of knowing God is faith. As long as we are in the flesh, we must attain God through his gleams in creation (Sir 17:8), including other men and, above all, Jesus. In Jesus, doubtless, God is uniquely present; but no presence of God to men apart from creatures is possible. The formula "one person in two natures" is not itself incompatible with the epistemology sketched on p. 260 but certain images that it conjures up are:

The offending images hang together with a dualistic view of man, sundering two factors not only as regards the knowing subject, but also as regards the known object. There is a connection between that dualism in which the soul as seat of intellectual activities is distinct from the material body, and that dualism which separates God from the creation in which he manifests himself. The latter dualism claims God can be attained directly in bypassing the material creation, and in Christ there is present at the side of a human nature also a divine person as the proper subject. Against that, I claim that man's intellectual light must be seen in function of the undivided cosmic reality which man is, just as God's presence to man must be seen in function of the undivided cosmic reality in which he reveals himself: the universe, man, Christ. Renouncing psychic dualism demands also renouncing Christological dualism. But just as the overcoming of psychic dualism need not entail the downgrading of that human value expressed in the biblical "image of God" and "child of God," so also the overcoming of Christological dualism need not jeopardize the place both in creation and in soteriology due to Christ as Son of God.

These lines give us the clearest formulation of the alleged parallel between the unity of principle of spiritual and material activities in man, and the unity of principle between human and divine activities in the man Jesus. The statement seems carefully formulated, moderate, and convincing. At most one might sniff something ominously like pantheism in the elimination of duality between God and creation. To this Hulsbosch could doubtless reply with Teilhard that it is no more pantheistic than Paul's "God will be all in all."[16]

The next thing to take up is the implication of "the Son" as Jesus' own name for himself. First we must accept the recently vindicated authenticity of the three passages Mk 13:32, Mk 12:6, and Mt 11:27.[17] The least we can conclude from these is that Jesus is not just a man like other men. But this does not exclude applicability of the term "Son" to the human subjectivity of Jesus. The question is whether he is Son and person in what he is as man, or apart from what he is as man. Christ is uniquely (Col 1:15) the "image of God" which all men are; it was never assumed that this revelation of God in the case of other men was founded in a subjectivity different from what man himself is as subject. Jesus too is *this* revelation of God in any case. Moreover, when we say that God from eternity brings forth a Son like himself, this remains for us meaningless speculation unless we can point to this being-Son in a created expression available to us.

In current discussion of the divinity of Christ there is a panic-stricken concern to safeguard his uniqueness; but precisely when the divinity is located outside his humanity, the man Jesus risks being reduced to the level of any other man (p. 262). Jesus taught us to serve God by serving our fellow men, and thus his own earthly life becomes emphasized. His cry of abandonment on the Cross is what men of today find the most relevant thing about him in the whole Bible. The resurrection can nowadays be less easily taken in stride than heretofore; Paul's "preach a crucified Christ, scandal to the Jews and folly for the pagans" becomes now "preach a risen Christ, scandal for Christians, and impossibility for scientists." The unwillingness of our contemporaries to admit that the transcendent divine and the created human are united in one man results in their seeing the man Jesus as a *mere* man; and to this snare orthodox Catholics also fall prey if they interpret sacrosanct formulas to mean that the divinity of Jesus is something apart from his manhood. Hulsbosch (p. 263) formally rests this part of his case; one might show in Scripture a solid foundation for his more acceptable insight into the traditional formula.

Against the claim that revelation and created reality are identical, the objection may be raised that until man is present there can be no revelation But, in fact, even vanished primordial reality leaves traces for man to perceive later. God's highest revelation is in Jesus, "true God and true man"; but if we put this in the equally valid form "true God and true creature," we see how creation unreservedly is revelation. Every creature reveals God by what it is itself, and of course in no higher degree than what corresponds to its own reality. Just as the individual reveals itself more in its voice than in its hair, so God is revealed in Christ as center of the whole creation and in each creature in the measure of its value. By looking on Christ in unrealistic isolation, we have been tempted to consider his divinity something apart from his human creaturehood. But Christ is "Light of Light" precisely insofar as he is created man. We may feel that Hulsbosch's line of thought is here dependent upon an acceptance of the Scotist "cosmic Christ," which was the subject of a massive research in my Teilhard volume and also in a paper for the 1966 Scotist congress at Oxford.

Our World Needs God's Concursus

Hulsbosch approaches (p. 264) the theme of another major chapter of my volume. "The Christological dilemma is not only that we have regarded Christ as too isolatedly taken in himself. We have also accustomed ourselves to regard the creation too isolatedly. We confess that God created the world, but to make contact with the world we feel no further need of God." This is the pendant of a parallel absurdity in current theology manuals that Rahner repeatedly pillories. We have irresponsibly been willing to give up the direct and paramount influence of God in the production of our bodies, as the price we had to pay for keeping him as the producer of our souls.[18] Concursus is the sound and traditional Catholic doctrine which shows how the immediacy of creation's dependence upon God extends far *beyond* the production of "souls," but does not appear *differently* in their case.[19]

Hulsbosch admits that in saying that Christ is nothing "other" than man, he appears a heretic in the eyes of those who have the habit of looking upon creation in isolation. From that standpoint they are even undoubtedly right in making him out a heretic. But he claims to elude such a charge because for him "the divine worth of Christ shines out in the fact that he as creature reveals the Father." Philip wanted to see the Father directly, but Jesus told him: "He who sees me, sees the Father" all he can (p. 265). "Death of God" means ultimately a blighting dualistic outlook which no longer sees the

world as the presence of God but as the simple effect
of an absent God. By regarding Christ as the revelation
of the Father, we see the divine dimension rooted in the
Creator but expressed in the created dimension which
is the man Christ. "Dimensions" here means not parts or
juxtaposed realities, but a single reality seen from two
viewpoints. It is perhaps a bit surprising that Hulsbosch
does not choose to advert to the identity between the
etymology of "dimension" and his own earlier citation
from Cyril, whereby God in himself is in the "infinite
measure" or rather complete lack of limit, while in Christ
he is received or revealed in human *measure*.

"I can call Christ a creature, and then say that he is
man: I can call Christ revelation of God, and then say
that he is God." When Jesus says "He who sees me, sees
the Father," this implies that he as a distinct person is
revelation of the Father. But such "distinctness of person"
is to be sought in the human subjectivity of Jesus rather
than in a pre-existent divine person. Hulsbosch acknowl-
edges that in this he has come around to essential agreement with an article of Schoonenberg that he had pre-
viously questioned.[20] But he does not take up here an
objection that his wording here of itself arouses. If "I
can call Christ revelation of God, and then say that he
is God," and if I must also say that *every* creature in
its own lesser measure is revelation of God, then must
I not end up by calling the whole creation and every
other creature God also? How are we to evade what
Baur made of Kant against Schleiermacher: by Christ
we mean ideal man, man-as-such; and this is not fully
realized in any one man; "the historical Jesus cannot
be so identical with the God-man idea as to exclude its
expressions in other men"?[21] This seems to be a kind
of reverse of Barth's statement: "Precisely God's *deity*
when rightly understood includes his humanity. . . . This

is a Christological statement. . . . Our question must be 'who or what is God *in Jesus Christ?'* "[22] A reply might well be sought in our notion of the mystical Christ, somehow taking up the whole creation in himself as head. But Hulsbosch, in fact, faces up to this objection in a different way and at a later point: "Jesus is revelation of God in virtue of the unique knowledge by which he is bound to the Father. But this does not deny that the whole creation as creation of God possesses a divine dimension, as the *OT* shows especially regarding God's wisdom as a divine presence in creation: Prv 8:22 ff.; Ps 139:17 f.; 19:2 ff.; 92:5 ff." (p. 266).

Revised View of Pre-existence

Granting that revelation of the Son can occur only via Christ as man, the problem still remains whether it is a pre-existent Son who reveals himself: "the glory which I had with God before the world began" (Jn 17:5), the bread given from heaven. But Hulsbosch sees Jesus possessing this glory precisely as man seen and heard by men. Being truly God as well as truly man in his human subjectivity, to it also he can ascribe pre-existence by a kind of retrojection, much as when we say "The Chief Justice was born in 1908": the person as we know him now is rightly named as subject of those activities which preceded. The divine dimension of Jesus is truly divine, and therefore from eternity. Since the revelatory divinity of Christ does not exclude that of the whole creation, the pre-existence of Christ is paralleled by that of (personified) Wisdom in the fashioning of the world (Prv 8:22). "The harmony of the universe, the complexity and distinctiveness of creatures, the laws of nature and the wisdom of man able to give the right orientation to his subsistence, are all clarified by the Wisdom of God everywhere present and instructing men" (p. 267); the *NT* authors reflect this *OT* view in ascribing cosmic significance to Christ's redemptive act (Rom 8:23).

If we need say no more of Christ than that as man he is revelation of the Father and thus true God, then what are we to say of the Spirit? Paul, in fact, calls the glorified Christ himself "a quickening spirit" (1 Cor 15:45, echoed in fifteen texts); but in Jn 16:7 and Acts 2:33 Christ and the Spirit are distinguished. At any rate, the Spirit is never subject of crucifixion and resurrection. Comparing Trinitarian texts like Eph 1:17 and Gal 4:6, Hulsbosch concludes: "We may say that Christ is revelation of the Father but can be known as such only through the Spirit; and this amounts to saying that the Spirit is the revelatory dimension of Christ" (p. 268). The term "revelatory dimension," while in one aspect here identical with "the Spirit," is said by Hulsbosch to take the place of "divine nature" in his new-sounding formula "Christ is nothing other than man revealing God, and therefore truly God." Christology can thus be rewritten significantly, substituting "Holy Spirit" for "divine nature" wherever it occurs. Spirit and Christ are two names for the same reality, since the Spirit is God as revealing himself in the form which is Christ. If from Christ you think away the Spirit, you think away everything.

But how can true divine sonship be retained, Hulsbosch asks (p. 269), if the divinizingly revelatory function is shared in gradual degree with all the other creatures? Our dogma is that creatures are sons by adoption and Christ is the Son by nature; and this tolerates no mere gradation. But dogma also insists that Christ is true man and therefore true creature, thus only in degree distinct from other creatures; his "grace of headship" is a created grace. Hence theology has always been perplexed about how the relation of the Son to the divine Father could be expressed in an *opus ad extra* effected by the

Trinity without distinction of persons.[23] Hulsbosch sees in the innovation proposed by him nothing which does violence to the fundamental fact that Christ in the created grace of his humanity is center of the Christological salvation-order. What he objects to is making the personal subjectivity of Christ a preexistent divine reality distinct from anything human.

The whole *NT* attests that Jesus stands in a different relation to God than *other* men. As unique created revelation of God, Jesus is man in a unique way. Less felicitously in the traditional Christology, Christ's humanity, though "of infinite dignity," is reduced to the common level of any other humanity (p. 270). That is not right. Especially as glorified (1 Cor 15:45 f.), but even in teaching men to say "Our Father," Jesus sets himself apart from other men in his dealing with the Father.[24] The Father makes himself known to Jesus otherwise than to the disciples. The greatest anguish of Jesus was not his betrayal by men but his abandonment by the Father. That sonship which he possessed embryonically from his conception Hulsbosch sees him "turning in" by obedience and death, in order to receive it to the fullest as the New Man by the sending of the Spirit. Hence the Infancy Narratives can never be demythologized of their essential content (p. 271): "Jesus is procreated by the Spirit, and *therefore* will be called Son of God" (Lk 1:35). Any difficulty in God's thus finding expression in the creation ever vivified by him can be seen only by the inveterate dualist who mutters: "Let God stay in his spiritual sphere, the material is our domain." "Our Father, which art in heaven, comma, stay where you are."[25] Against this Hulsbosch claims that revelation, for the simple reason that it itself comprises the whole of cosmic reality, can never involve violation of nature's laws.

Hulsbosch's final paradox is that in the *NT* Jesus is

never the brother of men, yet men are his brothers.[26]
His earthly life cannot be evaluated alone but only in relation to the completion which he has attained as firstling
of creation. Confession of God's transcendence remains
an empty word if we think we know all about the world
around us. But the physicist with whom Hulsbosch began
confesses that what we truly know about atoms is equivalent to ignorance of what matter really is ultimately. No
less modest should be our assurance as to whether we
have the last word about God's mode of revealing himself
in the universe around us, in men, and in Christ. "Yah-
weh's works are unfathomable; where man thinks he has
done, he has only begun" (Sir 18:6 f.).

Schoonenberg Further on Pre-existence

We have already noticed the relatively mild reserves
of Schoonenberg regarding the elimination of "hypostatic." He shows much more concern with the invalidity
of "pre-existence" in his general critique (p. 289). Hulsbosch speaks pastorally to the man of today, but does
he do justice to Scripture and tradition? To Scripture,
yes, certainly. There Jesus is called Christ and Son of
God because in him God definitively or eschatologically
speaks his word to us and offers us his salvation. This
Christology uses what has been called "the revelation-
model instead of the two-nature model."[27] Just bypassing
Chalcedon cannot be equated with being confronted with
two natures and then rejecting one of them, the divine.

No Christian, however, can ignore the Church's tradition in revising the formulas for revealed data. Hulsbosch
revered that tradition, in seeking to transpose it from an
old epistemology to a more contemporary one. In this
Schoonenberg hopes to support him explicitly, and better, by setting forth the issues in his differing hermeneutic,
of which Hulsbosch has in fact taken notice.[28] That arti-

cle is thus summarized (p. 290). It is a question whether our faith requires the Son's pre-existence or subsistence as divine person before or apart from his Incarnation. This is not equivalent to doubting that a divine hypostasis of the Word was present in the Christ of human form; and Schoonenberg is still reserving judgment as to whether a divine hypostasis, ordered to but really distinct from his humanity, constitutes the man Jesus.

Pre-existence of the Son from eternity alongside the Father and the Holy Spirit independently of the Incarnation has always been a tenet no less of the Orthodox and the Reformed than of the Catholic Christology. Calvin made the divinity of Christ something transcendent even to his humanity and "outside" it. But whether we say "outside" or "before," the implication is neither temporal nor spatial, but merely that the subsistence of the Son is independent of the Incarnation. This implies the "two-nature pattern" which Hulsbosch sweeps away. Schoonenberg is ready to follow him, but somewhat more hesitantly.

Can we really say that pre-existence is irrelevant to us? Admittedly we know nothing of God except what is revealed to us in creatures; but we there experience him as transcendent. By our very inability to say what God is, we confess his transcendence (p. 291). It is not a priori excluded that in some similar way we detect and confess in the man Jesus an "inexpressible" element which would equally mean his transcendent or pre-existent divine Sonship. Far from being irrelevant, an acceptance of this position would require a return to the Cappadocian Trinitarian formula in preference to the speculations of Augustine and Thomas. So the question must be posed. And having been posed, its pre-existence-alternative must be rejected. Or at least, without pronouncing upon what may or may not be the Trinitarian state of affairs within God himself, Schoonenberg can affirm that, *as known by theology* and within the person-categories of our psychology, there was no person of the Son independent of the Incarnation.

Obvious barriers to pre-existence lie in the "two-layer" and "one plus one making two" fallacies. The situation which would have resulted in Christ has been, not ineptly, called schizophrenia. In less dramatic terms, we cannot take seriously as historical reality a Jesus growing in knowledge if his only person already knew everything. His human freedom too would be unintelligible. Thomism escapes these hazards by claiming that even in the Trinity there is only common and not personal knowledge and willing.[29] A better answer would be that the divine knowledge or will never stands beside the human like one plus one, but activates it (p. 292). Still, the difficulty is not thereby solved.

In the supposition of pre-existence we throw the dualism back into the divine nature itself, where the Son in relation to any possible "works *ad extra*" is undifferentiated from the Father and yet simultaneously identical with the creature whose sole person he is, and even center of the whole creation. To reply that he is this in the way proper to the Second Person, in their dependence on the Father, does not diminish either the transcendence of his relation to a work *ad extra,* or the *creaturely* relation which the person of Jesus has to the (rest of) creation.

Even more clearly: as goal of creation, the pre-existent Son would have to be the Thou toward which we yearn, though he is mediator; He would be offerer and receiver, a virtual duality. "I cannot accept a Son who creates his own humanity, or a man who is priest toward his own divinity" (p. 293). Morever, pre-existence without relation to Incarnation or Pentecost is. tritheism: God would be three times his conscious self.

Thomism evades this difficulty by claiming to make within the Trinity real "persons" of what is nothing more than the conciliar "hypostases": no trace of consciousness or freedom is found either in Boethius' "individual substance of rational nature" or in Richard of St. Victor's "incommunicable existence of a nature."[30] The Thomist Son and Spirit are terms of God's immanent knowing and willing, but do not themselves as persons know or will. This was a sly maneuver to avoid three gods, but disillusioning to whoever has an esteem for what "person" means. Braun's effort to save both by distinguishing "being otherwise" from "being other" is unconvincing.[31] What he rightly sets forth about dialogue among the persons agrees with Schoonenberg's notion of the Father's dialogue with Jesus or with the Spirit in us.

Lair of the NT Pre-existence Formulas

Schoonenberg takes up what Scripture says of Son's pre-existence (p. 274). The NT dictums echo the Jewish apocalyptic literature, rabbinic lore, and the Wisdom literature of the OT.[32] The former two groups envision the pre-existent as a *man* up there with God: apocalyptic reckons with "a Son of Man hidden to be revealed," and the rabbis with a Messiah pre-existing really only in soul, but otherwise only ideally in God's plan. But the real basis for the NT Jesus' pre-existence is the *divine* wisdom present with God from or before the moment of creation, in Jb 28:20-28; Bar 3:32-38; Prv 8:22-31; Sir 1:4-9; 24: 3–22; and Wis 7:25; 9:9–11 The bubbling rock in the desert which Philo calls wisdom is called Christ in 1 Cor 10:4. Also, Jn 12:41 and 8:56 show Isaiah and Abraham seeing Christ, though this can mean simply that they saw his eventual place in the plan of salvation. Similarly, the Christ in whom "all things have their being" (1 Cor 8;6; Col 1:15 f.; Heb 1:2) hints at a pre-existence before creation, but only in the sense assigned to pre-existence in the Wisdom literature; the same is true of John's

Prologue insofar as it combines the Greek *Logos* with the Jewish *Memra* (p. 295).

Outright assertion of the pre-existent Christ does indeed flicker in Eph 1:4 and Jn 17:5; less clearly Jn 8:58 and Phil 2.[33] Moreover, all *NT* formulations of the Incarnation seem to imply that the Word was already *there* to "become" flesh. But none of these texts really describes a previous existence of Christ in himself within the Godhead. They are all compatible with a divine *decision* of the Incarnation from eternity, even if this decreed future *Person* is personified as in Wisdom. At any rate, this in some sense pre-existent Reality is never credited with any personal activtity; his whole reality is to "be there," upholdingly (Heb 1:3), or really to "be coming." But this was enough to overpower the Hellenistic thought-world.[34] Justin's *Apology* 2, 10, with overtones of Plato and the Stoa, describes God's Logos communicated partially to all men but totally to Christ. Yet neither he nor Hippolytus nor Tertullian ever considers this divine Word or Spirit in Christ other than in relation to the Incarnation. From their formulas, ambiguity was bound to arise as to how Christ differed from the Prophets, who also had their share in God's spirit; thus came the adoptionism of Paul of Samosata, which was condemned by Cyril and others in language that, ironically enough, would likewise reject Nicaea's *homoousios.*

Novatian is the first in the West to assert unequivocally that the Son has a "substance" of his own and is born of the Father before all time: "otherwise the Father would not always have been Father" (*Trinity* 31; Schoonenberg, p. 297). The same argument is pressed by Origen to show that God must have always been Creator; so before the material creation there must always have been created spirits (destined eventually to be united as souls with human bodies), with the Logos and Holy Spirit above them. These pre-existent souls have vanished from theology's purview, but we must not overlook how the pre-existent Logos was no more pre-existent than they, and was related to the eventual created bodily beings. Some of the Church Fathers transformed these Origenist pre-existent souls into angels, in order to give the pre-existent Christ something to do in shepherding such creatures.

Origen's thoughts fathered equally Arianism and the orthodox reactions against it (p. 298). But pre-existence did not find its way into the Nicene Creed (*DS* 125), only into an anathema subjoined to it (*DS* 126), which was adopted at Constantinople (*DS* 150) and thus got into the Credo of the Mass. But all these formulas, plus *DS* 272, 294, 301, 500, 3025, leave open *some* possibility that the existence of God as Son from all eternity is in relation to his eventual human nature. However, after Nicaea and Constantinople, formulations taken from Origen and Hippolytus lost their emphasis on what had been originally paramount: the Logos is such in relation to creation, the Son is such with relation to his Incarnation (p. 300). *"Pater generat Filium incarnando eum,"* or *"ab aeterno generat Filium incarnandum."*

A nonlinear view of God's eternity finds the Incarnation equally present to him at, after, or before creation. Thus the pre-existent-Son formula is correct in implying that there never was a "not yet" within God; he could not become "more God" with the passage of time, but with the passage of *our* time he could become more *God for us*. In this connection the two Dutch pioneers are in agreement against the bulk of scholastic speculation that the *relations* between God and creation are *real*, not only from creatures toward God but from God toward creatures.[35] The *dependence* which this implies in God is a purely logical one, therefore in our minds rather than in him, though the relation is really in him. Scholasticism itself admits real relations *within* God of the independent toward the dependent, namely, of the origin-Father toward the originated Son and Spirit. And God's anger and joy may be anthropomorphisms, but his love for us (1 Jn 4:8, 16) is not an *ens rationis* (p. 302).

Schoonenberg takes calmly in stride the fact that these real relations of God to creatures presuppose that there are, in a real but divine way, change and becoming in God. St. Thomas was recently shown to have unvaryingly denied such change.[36] But he patently means only such change as implies imperfection in the mutant, or any pantheistic evolutionism (*DS* 126, 3001, 3024). Neither Thomas nor Ottolander really faces the question of whether without imperfection God really changes in his real relations to his creatures. But Rahner has faced and answered this with the formula "God *others* (changes, *ändert)* himself on the Other."[37] True, God is not pantheistically evolving; but neither is he any kind of an unmoved mover. Whoever cannot reconcile that with God's perfection had better re-examine whether he is hampered by a too-human notion of perfection with too little scope for divine freedom (p. 303). It is no Sabellian "three-hat" Godhead to say that God *becomes* trinity (from eternity, or rather *in* his eternity) by communicating himself totally to, and being present in, the man Jesus as Word, and the Church as Spirit.

Hypostatic Unity Rather than Union

We have thus surveyed the whole of both the positive presentation of a "new Christology" by Hulsbosch, and Schoonenberg's support of it chiefly on the basis of re-appraising "pre-existence." From Schillebeeckx we have excerpted chiefly his uneasiness about evolutionism and about how the basically valid Chalcedon notion of hy-postasis has been manhandled. We may now conclude by according due emphasis to Schillebeeckx' own revised and constructive notion of "hypostatic *unity* rather than *union.*" In the primitive Christology, he says (p. 280), historical man Jesus himself, though not beyond or out-side his faith-relation to the primitive community, is experienced eschatologically as the concrete forgiving nearness of God.

The record of this experience in the *NT* is revelation already illumined and thus interpreted by human historical faith. The portrayal of Christ in Paul is different from that in Mark or in John. The primitive community, inverting the order which seems natural to teachers of a later day, came to grips first and longest with the divine presence manifested in Jesus' public activity, only secondly with his person, and last of all with what his birth and youth must have been like. Chalcedon is just one more in a series whereby first Paul, then the Synoptics, then John had re-expressed, with the help of thought patterns cur-rent in each respective milieu (p. 281), the forgiving presence of God in the man Jesus. In terms like those of Hulsbosch we can hope to recapture and hold firmly that prime fact even if we thereby lose sight of some specific interpretations which had been found to be very suitable by those respective past ages. We must learn from recent rehabilitation of Church Fathers once branded heretical that even outright denial of a term like hypo-static union might be some man's way of clearing the deck for a renewed and deeper grasp of the mystery of Christ. Such a try must, of course, be tested against the *sensus ecclesiae,* by anguished reappraisal rather than blind hurling of anathemas.

In this spirit of respectful cosearching, Schillebeeckx feels he must serenely ask whether Hulsbosch's formula does full justice to the personal unity of Christ demanded by the whole Christian tradition and crystallized in 1 Cor 3:23: "Christ is of God." To be sure, God is in Christ only as the infinite measured by the finite, and we can never speak of God and man in him as one and one making two, any more than we can say that one and one make two as an expression of the fact that metaphysically God is more one with *every* single man than that man is one with himself. My being-myself and my being-creature are neither two components nor two partial aspects of my being, but both are equally expressions of my totality (p. 282). Whatever inescapable duality is involved in every creature's being simultaneously "of itself" and "of God" is only a low-key aspect of the unique way in which Paul says Christ is "of God." And by this norm Hulsbosch does indeed place the mystery of Christ in an exactly proper and biblical perspective.

But to vindicate this we have already been forced to spell out that not even the most relentless expulsion of dualism can escape admitting some kind of duality. Any man's "being-of-God" is the very constitutive of his "being-himself," his human subjectivity. So the "being-of-God" on a higher plane in Jesus *is* his human subjectivity. Jesus does thus, though uniquely, what every creature and especially every man does: "re-present (make present)" God by what the creature itself is. But to claim that we prove the *uniqueness* of Jesus' "making God present" *from* what we already know of the hypostatic union is to stand the history of revelation on its head. First and proximately and from the *NT* data we know that Jesus had a unique way of "making God present just by being the man he was," and *from this* the reasoning Church was able to grope toward her hypostatic formula.

"And here I must part company with Hulsbosch," Schillebeeckx says (p. 283), "because I claim rather that the dogmatic confession of hypostatic union never was meant to express anything other than the implications of Jesus' unique mode of being man, a uniqueness which would have to remain a mere meaningless word unless the hypostatic formula had been found." The dogma formulates God's absolute and forgiving presence in Christ, which *is* the hypostatic union itself. It does not follow that we have to swallow all the secondary and too-dualistic speculations with which the dogmatic formula has been escorted down through history.

In the case of Jesus, God did not merely "creatively posit" or infuse the being of a particular human subjectivity as he does for every man, but he creatively posited this special human subjectivity as his own. This is what ought to be called the "hypostatic unity." Preference of unity to union is here relegated by Schillebeeckx to a footnote comprising one half of one percent of the total of his article, but it looms into a massive six percent of the brief summary in English which he himself contributes on p. 288. The summary there wholly bypasses the following much more fascinating sidelight: His special way of being man involves also a special *mandate* for Jesus—just as the ordinary way of being man is always a mandate, a vocation which the man is commissioned to work out in his historical situation. When Jesus says "I" to the Father, it is *this man* who is speaking, not a subjectivity lying somewhere outside and distinct from the humanity. So *instrumentum conjunctum,* "tool hooked on," is an unacceptable paraphrase of the true, valid, dogmatic formula of hypostatic unity. The nature is never a tool of the person, but is the content of the person and his mode of being and acting (p. 284). We can say Jesus is the human way of being God, but we cannot say Jesus is the divine way of being man. "Mode of being" indicates nature, and the nature of the man Jesus is by definition human and not divine. This mystery is possible only because in no system of counting is any man ever "one" next to God in such a way that along with God he makes up "two." Nor is "human nature" ever a number one beside a number two which is "divine nature": God encompasses and includes whatever else there is. Finally, the man Jesus, being *in* his manhood Son of God by power of the Spirit, is the *personal* revelation-form of the God who is three in persons.

Knowledge of Absolute Need Not Be Absolute

Second, or perhaps rather as root of his above disagreement with Hulsbosch, Schillebeeckx focuses his dismay at reducing Christ's unique mode of being man to the procedure of creation itself. This is presented as a sort of corollary of the correct observation that the revelatory character of any creature can be no greater than the creature itself is. But we detect an ambiguity in the fact that "creative" is a term which can be applied to *any* activity of God, even including redemption. God *makes* men and things be in such and such a particular mode, and to that extent they are revelation of God in whatever they are or do. In this sense the uniqueness of the man Jesus, this "new way of being man," is also a new creation. Hence, however oddly, Augustine hit the nail on the head when he said that Christ's humanity was not first created and then assumed but "created by the very fact of being assumed"[38] (p. 285).

The creation which in that case occurs is the act of setting a man in hypostatic unity with God. As a person distinct from the Father, the personal man Jesus is the revelation of the Father; and the basis of that distinction of persons is not the "pre-existent divine Son," as Hulsbosch rightly says, but the human subjectivity of Jesus. In a summary (p. 288) Schillebeeckx spells out even more clearly in English: "This unique mode of being-man therefore must imply a Trinity in God himself, even if one should feel forced to abandon the idea of 'pre-existence' as an illusory concept, due to our essentially human, historical way of approaching reality." There is nothing quite like that sentence explicitly in the Dutch. Moreover, even in Hulsbosch's formulas which Schillebeeckx favors and adopts, it is not clear why the lesser revelation of God, which is contained in every man and every creature, should not simultaneously produce a lesser Trinity.

This difficulty is promptly faced in a more roundabout way. The human subjectivity of Jesus is indeed the basis of distinction in person between the man Jesus and the Father. Yet, against Hulsbosch, Schillebeeckx cannot explain the absolute uniqueness of this man and the fact that he is God's absolute nearness otherwise than with the words "hypostatic" and "consubstantial," *homoousios*. This man is the *personal* revelation-form of the Father. If you conjure away the hypostatic unity, the absoluteness of Jesus' human uniqueness is taken away. He would then be only one in a row of religious geniuses who have in fact brought men nearer to God.

Though Hulsbosch rightly holds that a reality that we do not know is irrelevant for us, and that Scripture does no more than call *this man* Son of God, still the further conclusion that "we too can say no more about it" seems to Schillebeeckx to smuggle in some epistemological presumptions which are neither evident nor widely shared. Let us grant that Merleau-Ponty was right, and that "our knowledge of an absolute" discerned behind shifting situations has in our tradition too often been confused with "an absolute type of knowledge." The absolute ever more evades our grasp, yet ever anew beckons it. Though the created reality of Jesus must forevermore remain outset-point for clarifying his uniqueness, still the very uniqueness of the Sonship of this man can turn out to be precisely the revelatory form of the Father (p. 286). The Absolute in him gives to us in the form of a fellow man.

We know no more about the divine Son, it is true, than what the man Jesus reveals; but also no less. It is no "essentialism" to insist that the divine hypostasis is relevant to us insofar as the man Jesus is relevant to us. This hypostasis is not beyond but in the man whom Scripture calls as man the Son of God. "Jesus experiences himself in presence of the Father as Son and, on the basis of this human experience sees himself as coming from the Father," Schillebeeckx finds Hulsbosch saying rightly. But an ordinary man's expressing himself to his fellow men and thereby revealing something of the creative God, is an altogether different thing from God's own expressing of himself personally in every utterance of the autonomous free man Jesus. This has always been the explanation of the human uniqueness of Jesus offered by the tradition of our faith. Hulsbosch has not sufficiently stressed that this explanation of God's absolute and forgiving presence in Jesus "must be ultimately a superstructure" (*dat deze duiding louter een bovenbouw zou zijn*), not a mere explication of the experience of Christ's unique personality. What the man Jesus says is personal revelation of the selfhood of God. In this case, every psychological insight (*anthropologische zegging*) is theological too, and every theological dictum also inextricably conveys something about human psychology.

What Hulsbosch has rightly said against the "two natures" as a sort of one plus one has derailed us. He could have nuanced it and thus saved the essential, instead of throwing out the hypostatic-union formula, at least in the form in which it has become spelled out. Anyway, he does keep the essential of it as long as he insists that Jesus in his human awareness has "an experience of God essentially (and not merely in degree) divergent" from that of other men. This way of viewing things admits that the essential otherness is present from the moment of Jesus' conception "through the Spirit of God."

Schillebeeckx concludes (p. 287) by adverting to Bousset's merit in purging theology from the notion of Christ as a "demigod" who "doubles for God."[39] Along with this came a fear that Christocentrism needlessly complicates the directness of man's simple *OT* approach to God.[40] Rohde thought he had simplified Christology by his thesis that Jesus was just an ordinary man who by his ascension became "Son of God."[41] Well, simplicity is often a pledge of truth and richness; but it can also be a token of scantiness. Sure enough, it complicates things to regard Jesus anthropomorphically as a middleman we have to go through to get to another *man*. But Thüsing has rightly seen in Paul that God's creative Glory can so appear in Christ that he promotes instead of hindering the goal "that God may be all in all."[42] This Pauline and more deeply Johannine vision of a Jesus "all on God's side and yet all on man's side" is what the Church has called "hypostatic unity."

CONCLUSIONS[43]

1) Strict unity of God and man in Christ, as of the soul and body in man, is a primary datum of revelation which has become progressively neglected in theologizing.

2) Jesus Christ has always been *known* to be man, real as a thing we can really know, but *confessed* to be Son of God, as a thing which is mysterious and ever beckons us toward better understanding.

3) Revelation is inextricably bound up with the meaningfulness of human existence. Formulas which genuinely block the intellect of modern man enshrine a truth which by patient effort can be more acceptably reformulated.

4) Chalcedon's formula of two natures and one person in Christ but three persons and one nature in the Trinity

uses "person" without implication of separate cognitive (self-) awareness, in a way which is incompatible with modern psychology and the universal way of speaking.

5) Just as there are facets of the divine being which will simply remain irrelevant to the beatified creature viewing, so there is in Jesus a creaturely human awareness of the God to whom he is in a special or rather unique relationship.

6) When it is said "Jesus is, besides man, also God," such an "also God" cannot form part of the salvation reality. The divine nature of Jesus is relevant to the saving mystery only insofar as it alters and elevates the human nature.

7) The very thing which Chalcedon most sought to safeguard is destroyed if we interpret it as meaning that the divinity of Christ is a separate thing from his humanity, a "one plus one making two."

8) The same intolerable "one plus one making two" has crept into theologians' viewing of the *soul,* which they meanwhile claim to be the *form* or structural principle of the "body" (meaning really *whole material person*).

9) The living being is not matter plus life, but living matter; man is not body plus soul, but animated body; Christ is not a human nature plus God, and not "God *assuming* a human nature," but God-*become*-man.

10) Pre-existence of the divine nature of Christ as Son *apart* from its (foreseen) Incarnation is hinted in the *NT* only in Eph 1:4 and Jn 17:5, but is plausibly traceable to the nonhypostatic Wisdom of Prv 8:27 and the rabbinic Pre-existent "*man* up there with God" and apocalyptic "Son of Man hidden in order to be revealed."

11) The "Pre-existent Christ" is really due to Origen, and equally fostered Arianism and the orthodox reactions against Arianism, but in Origen is linked with assurance that there must have been an equally pre-existent created

universe of souls or spirits to relate to Christ. Stripping our revealed datum of its Origenist accretions leaves open the formula "The Father generates the Son by incarnating him . . . from eternity he generates the incarnand Son."

12) In first saying that the Son has a "substance" of his own and "was born of the Father before all time, otherwise the Father would not have been Father," Novatian in the West implies rightly that there never was a "not yet" within God, wrongly that there was an "already" *preceding* some event of human time.

13) Because God is necessarily related to time-bound changes at least in the walkabout humanity of Jesus, real relations must be admitted in God toward creatures, only not such relations as imply imperfection.

14) Cyril's formula "the human is the measure in which the divine appears in Christ" is compatible with the careful formulations of *Sum. theol.* 3, q. 3.

15) As Christ is the revelatory di-mension (= measure) of the Father, so the Spirit is the revelatory dimension of Christ.

16) The unique person of Jesus the God-man is an unfolding of possibilities which were somehow latent within matter itself, and were precisely by their *uniqueness* distinct from the mode in which material creation reveals God, and man is his image.

17) "He who sees me, sees the Father also" (Jn 14:11) as much as he *can,* must be our constant answer to an outlook which no longer sees the world as presence of God but as simple effect of an absent (dead) God.

18) Other affirmations of these three Dutch theologians, especially where they disagree and correct one another, are subject to rigorous appraisal; but even if eventually rejected, need not diminish the usefulness of the seventeen propositions focused above.

Notes

1. Ansfried Hulsbosch, "Jezus Christus, gekend als mens, beleden als Zoon Gods." *Tijdschrift voor Theologie* 6 (1966) 250.

2. E. Schillebeeckx, "Persoonlijke openbaringsgestalte van de Vader," *Tijdschrift voor Theologie* 6 (1966) 274.

3. R. North, *Teilhard and the Creation of the Soul* (Milwaukee, 1967), pp. 166, 225.

4. Hulsbosch, "De Kosmogenese van Teilhard de Chardin," *Annalen van het Thijmgenootschap* 47 (1959) 317 ff.

5. Schillebeeckx, *art. cit.,* p. 275.

6. Denzinger-Schönmetzer, *Enchiridion Symbolorum* (Freiburg, 1963), 902. Hereafter *DS.* On the anomaly and limitations of such a dogma, see pp. 223–226 of my *Teilhard and the Creation of the Soul.*

7. See *Teilhard and the Creation of the Soul,* p. 18.

8. Barnabas M. Ahern, "The Christian's Union with the Body of Christ in Cor, Gal, Rom," *Catholic Biblical Quarterly* 23 (1961) 199–209, invoking Cerfaux, Benoit, and especially J.A.T. Robinson, *The Body: A Study in Pauline Theology* (London, 1952) 52, n. 1: "One could heartily wish that the misleading and unbiblical phrase, the 'mystical' body, had never been invented."

9. Hulsbosch, in *De Bazuin* of Oct. 16, 1965, p. 5.

10. E. Gutwenger, "Het kennen van Christus," *Concilium* 41 (1966) 84–97; *Bewusstsein und Wissen Christi* (Innsbruck, 1960) p. 55; B. Lonergan, *De verbo incarnato* (2nd ed.; Rome, 1961) p. 273; *De constitutione Christi* (Rome, 1961) p. 83.

11. P. Schoonenberg, "Christus zonder tweeheid?" *Tijdschrift voor Theologie* 6 (1966) 289–306 at pp. 303 ff. The references to Rahner are on p. 302. Note that John Knox, *The Church and the Reality of Christ* (New York, 1962), p. 96, denies that any formula explaining the Incarnation as presence of some authentic human capability extraordinarily or absolutely in Jesus is as good as Chalcedon, though on p. 85, he approves "dynamic personal medium of God's saving action," as W. Norman Pittenger, *The Word Incarnate* (New York, 1959).

12. E. Schillebeeckx, "Het bewustzijnsleven van Christus," *Tijdschrift voor Theologie* 1 (1961) 227–250; further treated by Schoonenberg, *art. cit.,* p. 292.

13. A. Hulsbosch, "De hypostatische vereniging volgens den H. Cyrillus van Alexandrië" [*Quod unus sit Christus,* PG 75, 1289], *Studia catholica* 24 (1949) 65–94; *metra,* PG 75, 1320.

14. Cajetan on 3, q. 2, a.5:n.2, Leonine ed. 35A.

15. Willi Marxsen, dialogue with Bultmann and Käsemann in *Der Streit um die Bibel* (Gladbeck-W, 1965); *Anfangsprobleme der Christologie* (2nd ed.; Gütersloh, 1964); *Die Auferstehung Jesu als historisches und als theologisches Problem* (Gütersloh, 1965).

16. 1 Cor 15:28; see my *Teilhard and the Creation of the Soul,* pp. 111–116.

17. B.M.F. van Iersel, *"Der Sohn" in den synoptischen Jesusworten* (Leiden, 1961).

18. K. Rahner, *Hominisation* (New York, 1966), p. 22; *Erscheinungsbild* (Freiburg, 1959) p. 13.

19. *Teilhard and the Creation of the Soul,* pp. 240–259; but in the preface contributed by Rahner (p. xi), note his newer reserves to what he had earlier said about concursus.

20. A. Hulsbosch, *Werkgenootschap van katholieke theologen in Nederland, Jaarboek* 1963/64 (Hilversum, 1965), pp. 1,12 f.; P. Schoonenberg, "Over de Godmens," *Bijdragen* 25 (1964) 166–186.

21. Peter C. Hodgson, *Formation of Historical Theology: A Study of Ferdinand Christian Baur* (New York, 1966), pp. 46, 104.

22. Karl Barth, *The Humanity of God* (Richmond, 1960), pp. 46 f.

23. H. Lyons, "The Grace of Sonship," *Ephemerides theologicae Lovanienses* 27 (1951), 438–466, needfully correcting St. Thomas.

24. But note Raymond E. Brown, "Does the NT call Jesus God?" *Theological Studies* 26 (1965) 549: Where Jesus calls men his brothers in Jn 20:17, "We cannot accept the contention [that he] is making a careful (and theological) distinction between his own relationship to the Father and the relationship of his disciples to the Father." Reprinted in Brown's *Jesus, God and Man* (Milwaukee, 1968).

25. Jacques Prévert, cited in Gabriel Vahanian, *The Death of God* (New York, 1961) p. 55; see Rahner as cited in n. 18 above and in *Teilhard and the Creation of the Soul,* p. 233.

26. Hulsbosch seems to be here relying on Wilhelm Michaelis, "Prototokos," *Theologisches Wörterbuch zum Neuen Testament* 6 (Stuttgart, 1959) 879, and related essays of his focused in our exegesis of Col 1:15; *Teilhard and the Creation of the Soul,* p. 131.

27. John McIntyre, *The Shape of Christology* (London, 1966).

28. P. Schoonenberg, "Over de Godmens," *Bijdragen* 25 (1964) 166–186; "De eenheid van Christus en de preëxistentie van de Soon," *Werkgenootschaap van katholieke theologen in Nederland, Jaarboek* 1963/64 (Hilversum, 1965) pp. 92–111; discussion pp. 112–119.

29. See E. Schillebeeckx, "Het bewustzijnsleven van Christus," *Tijdschrift voor Theologie* 1 (1961) 227–250 at p. 242 f.

30. Aquinas, *Sum. theol.* 1, q. 29, a.1; 1, q. 29, a.3, ad 4m.

31. M. Braun, *Het geheim van het goddelijke persoonlijkheden* (Bruges, 1958).

32. Rudolf Schnackenburg, "Jesus Christus, II. Neutestamentliche Christologie," *Lexikon für Theologie und Kirche* 5 (2nd ed.; Freiburg, 1960) 934 ff. See now the lineup of texts (with 2 Cor 8:9, Heb 11:26, Ap 22:13 replacing Jn 12:41 and Eph 1:4, and 1 Enoch 48:3 replacing Baruch and Sirach)

in F. B. Craddock, *The Pre-Existence of Christ in the New Testament* (New York, 1968), called a "category once functional but now anachronistic."

33. André Feuillet, "L'Homme-Dieu considéré dans sa condition terrestre de Serviteur et de Redempteur," *Revue biblique* 51 (1942) 58–79.

34. J.N.D. Kelly, *Early Christian Doctrines* (3rd ed.; London, 1965) pp. 95–136.

35. So E. Schillebeeckx, "De zin van het menszijn van Jezus, de Christus," *Tijdschrift voor Theologie* 2 (1962) 127–172 at p. 130.

36. P. den Ottolander, *Deus immutabilis: Wijsgerige beschouwing over onveranderlijkheid en veranderlijkheid volgens de theo-ontologie van Sint Thomas en Karl Barth* (Assen, 1965), pp. 3–78.

37. K. Rahner, "Theos im NT"; "Probleme der Christologie," *Schriften zur Theologie* 1 (Einsiedeln, 1954), 125 ff. and 196 ff. Cf. F. Malmberg, *Über den Gottmenschen* (Basle, 1960), pp. 62–65.

38. *Against Arian Talk* (PL 42, 688).

39. Wilhelm Bousset, *Kyrios Christos: Geschichte des Christusglaubens von den Anfängen des Christentums bis Irenäus* (Göttingen, 1921), p. 150.

40. We might suggest here the relevance of Gabriel Vahanian's strange horror of "the Christic Man" as a parody of "the NT New Man" as keystone of that baneful "religiosity, which is to Faith what the Peeping Tom is to love; curiosity without involvement": *The Death of God* (New York, 1961), pp. 15, 67.

41. Eduard Rohde, "Gottesglaube und Kyriosglaube bei Paulus," *Zeitschrift für die neutestamentliche Wissenschaft* 22 (1923) 54 ff.

42. W. Thüsing, *Per Christum in Deum: Studien zum Verhältnis von Christozentrik und Theozentrik in den paulinischen Hauptbriefen* (Munster, 1965), p. 261.

43. The first seventeen propositions are all contained within the three Dutch articles, and seem to be sound and acceptable as there contained, though not everything there is sound and acceptable even in the judgment of the other two contributors.